1

WOULD YOU RATHER TRIP EVERY TIME YOU LOOKED LEFT, OR SNEEZE EVERY TIME YOU USED YOUR RIGHT HAND?

2

WOULD YOU RATHER HAVE FIVE OF YOUR TEETH PULLED OR HAVE TO BE BEST FRIENDS WITH YOUR LEAST FAVORITE PERSON?

3

WOULD YOU RATHER HAVE A NECK TWO FEET LONG OR HAVE EARS LIKE AN ELEPHANT?

4

WOULD YOU RATHER BE 7 FEET TALL AND REALLY WEAK, OR 3 FEET TALL AND STRONG AS AN OX?

5

WOULD YOU RATHER LOSE YOUR SIGHT AND SMELL OR YOUR HEARING AND TASTE?

Over 400 funny and thought provoking Would You Rather Questions 4 Everyone!

Don't forget the BONUS questions at the end of the book!

6

WOULD YOU RATHER BE ABLE TO SPRINT 1 MILE OR DO 100 PULL UPS WITHOUT BREAKING A SWEAT?

7

WOULD YOU RATHER LOSE YOUR HANDS OR YOUR FEET?

8

WOULD YOU RATHER HAVE TO SING EVERYTHING YOU SAID OUT LOUD OR BE MUTE?

9

WOULD YOU RATHER INCREASE YOUR ABILITY TO SMELL OR BE 5 TIMES STRONGER?

10

WOULD YOU RATHER HAVE TO CRAWL AROUND ON ALL FOURS FOR THE REST OF YOUR LIFE OR HAVE A TAIL LIKE A FOX?

11

WOULD YOU RATHER HAVE EIGHT ARMS OR EIGHT LEGS?

12

WOULD YOU RATHER LOOK REALLY WIMPY AND BE STRONG, OR LOOK REALLY STRONG AND BE WEAK?

13

WOULD YOU RATHER HAVE EYES SO BIG YOU LOOKED LIKE A CARTOON CHARACTER OR SPEECH BUBBLES THAT POPPED UP EVERY TIME YOU SAID ANYTHING?

14

WOULD YOU RATHER BE THE BEST ATHLETE IN THE WORLD BUT NOT VERY SMART, OR BE THE SMARTEST PERSON IN THE WORLD BUT BE CRIPPLED IN A WHEELCHAIR?

15

WOULD YOU RATHER LOSE THE ABILITY TO READ OR TO SPEAK?

16

WOULD YOU RATHER BE ABLE TO ONLY HEAR HIGH PITCHED SOUNDS OR LOW SOUNDS?

17

WOULD YOU RATHER NEVER BE ABLE TO STOP READING OR NOT KNOW HOW TO READ?

18

WOULD YOU RATHER STAND A WHOLE DAY IN 100 DEGREE WEATHER WEARING WINTER CLOTHES, OR IN - 20 DEGREES WEARING SUMMER CLOTHES?

19

WOULD YOU RATHER HAVE ONE VERY BEST FRIEND OR 100 "OKAY" FRIENDS?

20

WOULD YOU RATHER BE A JANITOR BUT MAKE $100,000 A YEAR OR HAVE YOUR DREAM JOB AND MAKE $20,000 A YEAR?

21

WOULD YOU RATHER HAVE TO WEAR ALLIGATOR SCALE PANTS OR A NATIVE AMERICAN HEADDRESS EVERYWHERE YOU WENT?

22

WOULD YOU RATHER FACE AN ARMY OF ALIENS WITH KNITTING NEEDLES OR AN ARMY OF ALIENS WIELDING METAL TONGS?

23

WOULD YOU RATHER HAVE TWO ITEMS OF YOUR CHOICE OR ONE PERSON OF YOUR CHOICE IF YOU WERE LOST IN THE WOODS?

24

WOULD YOU RATHER BE A FAMOUS OUTLAW ON THE RUN ALL THE TIME OR A NORMAL SHERIFF CHASING THE FAMOUS OUTLAW?

25

WOULD YOU RATHER COMPETE AND LOSE OR NEVER COMPETE BUT KNOW YOU WOULD WIN?

26

WOULD YOU RATHER BE RICH AND FAMOUS FOR SOMETHING YOU STOLE OR POOR BECAUSE SOMEONE TOOK CREDIT FOR SOMETHING IMPORTANT YOU INVENTED?

27

WOULD YOU RATHER LIVE THE REST OF YOUR LIFE IN A SUBMARINE OR A BLIMP?

28

WOULD YOU RATHER SURVIVE AN AVALANCHE OR A PLANE CRASH?

29

WOULD YOU RATHER BE ADORED WHILE YOU'RE ALIVE BUT HATED AFTER YOU DIE OR DESPISED WHILE YOU'RE ALIVE AND REVERED AFTER YOU DIE?

30

WOULD YOU RATHER LIVE IN THE BEST HOUSE IN THE WORST LOCATION, OR THE WORST HOUSE IN THE BEST LOCATION?

31

WOULD YOU RATHER HAVE A BIRD THAT WAS AFRAID OF HEIGHTS AND NEEDED TO BE CARRIED EVERYWHERE OR A RAT 5 FEET LONG?

32
WOULD YOU RATHER BE ALLERGIC TO ANIMALS OR HUMANS?

33
WOULD YOU RATHER VANDALIZE PEOPLE'S PROPERTY OR REPAIR PEOPLE'S VANDALIZED PROPERTY FOR A LIVING?

34
WOULD YOU RATHER MOW A FOOTBALL FIELD WITH SCISSORS, OR PICK UP POOP AT A DOG PARK WITH TWEEZERS?

35
WOULD YOU RATHER FIND A HIDDEN WORLD AND NOT BE ABLE TO TELL ANYONE ABOUT IT OR YOUR BEST FRIEND TELLS YOU ABOUT A HIDDEN WORLD BUT WON'T TAKE YOU TO IT?

36
WOULD YOU RATHER EVERYDAY BE HALLOWEEN OR EASTER?

37

WOULD YOU RATHER BE YOUR FAVORITE BOOK CHARACTER, OR BE FRIENDS WITH YOUR FAVORITE BOOK CHARACTER?

38

WOULD YOU RATHER LIVE IN YOUR FAVORITE BOOK OR HAVE YOUR FAVORITE BOOK CHARACTER LIVE IN THE REAL WORLD WITH YOU?

39

WOULD YOU RATHER BE FAMOUS FOR YOUR REALLY SMART GOLDFISH OR FOR BALANCING A SPINNING TOP ON YOUR HEAD?

40

WOULD YOU RATHER BE AN EXPERT AT SOMETHING USELESS, OR A COMPLETE NOOB AT SOMETHING USEFUL?

41

WOULD YOU RATHER BE CHASED BY AN EVIL DENTIST WITH PLIERS OR HAVE TO FIGHT THE HEAVYWEIGHT BOXING CHAMPION OF THE WORLD?

42

WOULD YOU RATHER LIVE IN A HUGE TREE HOUSE OR A HUGE CAVE?

43

WOULD YOU RATHER RIDE AROUND ON A RINO EVERYWHERE OR CAMEL?

44

WOULD YOU RATHER LIVE IN THE DESERT OR THE ARCTIC?

45

WOULD YOU RATHER HAVE TO DRESS LIKE A CLOWN EVERY DAY OR HAVE A CLOWN RANDOMLY PURSUE YOU FOR THE REST OF YOUR LIFE?

46

WOULD YOU RATHER TIGHTROPE OVER ICE COLD WATER OR OVER MUD?

47

WOULD YOU RATHER BE ABLE TO BREATHE UNDERWATER BUT BE EXTREMELY CLAUSTROPHOBIC OR BE ABLE TO FLY BUT BE TERRIFIED OF HEIGHTS?

48

WOULD YOU RATHER BE ABLE TO CLIMB UP A TREE LIKE A SQUIRREL OR PICK UP DOG POOP WITH YOUR MIND?

49

WOULD YOU RATHER BE A WORLD-FAMOUS SUPERHERO AND BE IN DANGER ALL THE TIME OR HAVE POWERS THAT YOU COULDN'T TELL ANYONE ABOUT?

50

WOULD YOU RATHER HAVE A COOL SUPERHERO POWER BUT BE MADE FUN OF BECAUSE YOU HAVE THE CORNIEST OUTFIT EVER OR HAVE A LAME SUPERHERO POWER BUT BE REALLY POPULAR BECAUSE YOU HAVE A REALLY COOL OUTFIT?

51

WOULD YOU RATHER BE ABLE TO TURN INTO A COCKROACH OR A LADYBUG?

52

WOULD YOU RATHER BE MAGNETIC OR REPEL EVERY LIVING THING?

53

WOULD YOU RATHER BE ABLE TO SPEAK TO BIRDS OR FISH?

54

WOULD YOU RATHER BE A CRIMINAL WITH THE POWER TO READ MINDS OR A POLICE OFFICER WITH THE POWER TO SEE THROUGH WALLS?

55

WOULD YOU RATHER ONLY YOUR ARMS COULD PASS THROUGH WALLS, OR BE INVISIBLE, EXCEPT FOR YOUR SKELETON?

56

WOULD YOU RATHER YOUR SUPERHERO SIDEKICK BE A PELICAN OR A SHARK?

57
WOULD YOU RATHER HAVE SKUNK POWERS OR PORCUPINE POWERS?

58
WOULD YOU RATHER BE ABLE TO SEE IN THE DARK OR BREATH UNDERWATER?

59
WOULD YOU RATHER SAVE ONE GOOD GUY OR KILL ONE BAD GUY IN SELF-DEFENSE IF YOU COULD TIME TRAVEL ONLY ONCE?

60
WOULD YOU RATHER GO BACK IN TIME AND CHOOSE A WINNING LOTTERY TICKET OR MEET YOUR ROLE MODEL AS A KID?

61
WOULD YOU RATHER LIVE 200 YEARS IN THE PAST OR FUTURE?

62

WOULD YOU RATHER GO BACK IN TIME AND LEARN UNDER SOME OF THE GREATEST MINDS IN HISTORY OR RULE ALONGSIDE THE GREATEST LEADERS?

63

WOULD YOU RATHER VISIT YOUR PERSONAL FAVORITE TIME IN HISTORY ONCE OR VISIT THE WORST TIMES IN HISTORY AS MANY TIMES AS YOU WANTED?

64

WOULD YOU RATHER GO BACK IN TIME AND ACCIDENTALLY BECOME BEST FRIENDS WITH HISTORY'S WORST PERSON OR MAKE A MISTAKE AND BE HATED BY HISTORY'S GREATEST PERSON?

65

WOULD YOU RATHER GO BACK IN TIME TO PREVENT THE BLACK PLAGUE OR GO INTO THE FUTURE AND BRING BACK THE CURE FOR CANCER?

66

WOULD YOU RATHER NOT EAT PIZZA FOR A WHOLE YEAR OR NEVER BE ALLOWED TO PUT SYRUP ON PANCAKES AGAIN?

67

WOULD YOU RATHER WIN A HOTDOG EATING CONTEST OR EARN MONEY FOR WINNING THE UGLIEST NOSE CONTEST?

68

WOULD YOU RATHER HATE FOOD SO MUCH THAT YOU HAD TO BE FORCE FED SO YOU COULD STAY ALIVE, OR BE IMMORTAL AND FORBIDDEN TO EAT ANYTHING?

69

WOULD YOU RATHER DRINK A WHOLE GLASS OF HOT SAUCE OR EAT A CUP OF SALT?

70

WOULD YOU RATHER BE A PROFESSIONAL CARTWHEELER OR WATER CHUGGER?

71

WOULD YOU RATHER HAVE EVERYTHING YOU PUT IN YOUR MOUTH TASTE LIKE CARDBOARD, OR FEEL LIKE STYROFOAM?

72

WOULD YOU RATHER WEAR AN ORANGE JUMPSUIT EVERYWHERE YOU WENT OR A CHECKERED LEPRECHAUN OUTFIT?

73

WOULD YOU RATHER LIE ON BED OF KNIVES FOR AN HOUR OR BE STRANGLED BY A SNAKE FOR 15 MINUTES?

74

WOULD YOU RATHER HAVE HUGE BUNNY EARS OR MONSTROUS BUNNY TEETH?

75

WOULD YOU RATHER HAVE A FAKE PERSONALITY THAT ATTRACTS LOTS OF FRIENDS, OR BE YOURSELF AND HAVE ONLY A FEW FRIENDS?

76

WOULD YOU RATHER LIVE IN THE WORLD OF YOUR LEAST FAVORITE MOVIE OR WATCH YOUR LEAST FAVORITE MOVIE EVERY WEEK FOR THE REST OF YOUR LIFE?

77
WOULD YOU RATHER HAVE A SQUEAKY MOUSE VOICE OR A DEEP VOICE LIKE A TUBA?

78
WOULD YOU RATHER HAVE A PIG NOSE OR RABBIT BUCK TEETH?

79
WOULD YOU RATHER HAVE THE WHOLE WORLD SPEAK A DIFFERENT LANGUAGE THAN YOU OR EVERY SINGLE PERSON HAD THEIR OWN LANGUAGE?

80
WOULD YOU RATHER HAVE TO WALK ON YOUR HAND EVERYWHERE YOU WENT OR HAVE TO SAY I SMELL EVERY HOUR?

81
WOULD YOU RATHER HAVE GILLS AND FINS OR CLAWS AND PAWS?

82

WOULD YOU RATHER BE A CRAZY CAT PERSON OR A CRAZY DOG PERSON?

83

WOULD YOU RATHER BE A LEGENDARY NINJA OR A TIME TRAVELING THIEF?

84

WOULD YOU RATHER BE PRESIDENT OF THE WORLD OR OWN THE MOON?

85

WOULD YOU RATHER RULE OVER ALL THE HUMANS OR ALL THE ANIMALS?

86

WOULD YOU RATHER ALL YOUR FOOD TASTE LIKE CHOCOLATE OR EVERYTHING YOU DRINK TASTES LIKE SWEETENED CONDENSED MILK?

87

WOULD YOU RATHER WOULD YOU RATHER BE FREEZING COLD ALL THE TIME OR ROASTING HOT?

88

WOULD YOU RATHER HAVE A NINJA BUNNY FOR A PET OR A TAME MOUNTAIN LION?

89

WOULD YOU RATHER BE A TROLL UNDER A BRIDGE OR A WITCH IN A CANDY HOUSE?

90

WOULD YOU RATHER BE BEST FRIENDS WITH SOMEONE FAMOUS OR BE FAMOUS?

91

WOULD YOU RATHER HAVE A MOHAWK TEN FEET TALL OR A BEARD TEN FEET LONG?

92

WOULD YOU RATHER HAVE A GREEN AFRO OR A SKULLET?

93

WOULD YOU RATHER HAVE NOSE HAIR THAT CAME DOWN TO YOUR CHIN OR FIVE INCH LONG CURLY EYEBROWS?

94

WOULD YOU RATHER SHOOT UP IN THE AIR EVERY TIME YOU FARTED OR TELEPORT A FEW BLOCKS AWAY EVERYTIME YOU BURPED?

95

WOULD YOU RATHER BE FORCED TO RUDELY STICK OUT YOUR TONGUE EVERY TIME SOMEONE SAID HI TO YOU YOU OR FART EVERY TIME YOU SHOOK HANDS?

96

WOULD YOU RATHER MOVE TO A NEW HOME EVERY YEAR OF YOUR LIFE OR STAY IN THE SAME PLACE YOUR WHOLE ENTIRE LIFE?

97

WOULD YOU RATHER RIDE AN OSTRICH EVERYWHERE YOU WENT OR HAVE A SKUNK THAT ONLY SPRAYED YOUR ENEMIES FOLLOW YOU EVERYWHERE YOU WENT?

98

WOULD YOU RATHER WEAR YELLOW OR TEAL FOR THE REST OF YOUR LIFE?

99

WOULD YOU RATHER CONTROL FIRE OR WATER?

100

WOULD YOU RATHER DIE AT 20 BUT ACCOMPLISH EVERYTHING YOU DREAMED OR LIVE TO BE 100 BUT HAVE AN AVERAGE LIFE WITH NO MAJOR ACCOMPLISHMENTS?

101

WOULD YOU RATHER ALWAYS BE TWENTY MINUTES LATE OR TWO HOURS EARLY?

102
WOULD YOU RATHER LOSE THE ABILITY TO TASTE OR LOSE THE ABILITY TO SMELL?

103
WOULD YOU RATHER BE IN JAIL FOR TEN YEARS OR LIVE IN A ZOO WITH A MONKEY FOR THE REST OF YOUR LIFE?

104
WOULD YOU RATHER BE MARRIED TO A PERSON WHO'S POOR, BUT SMART OR MARRY A PERSON WHO'S RICH, BUT DUMB?

105
WOULD YOU RATHER HAVE THE ABILITY TO TELEPORT TO YOUR DESTINATION ANYTIME OR STOP TIME FOR ONE HOUR PER DAY?

106
WOULD YOU RATHER SPEND THE REST OF YOUR LIFE LIVING IN A SHIP OR IN A JET PLANE?

107

WOULD YOU RATHER BE FAMOUS FOR DISCOVERING A NEW CREATURE OR FAMOUS FOR EXPLORING A PLANET?

108

WOULD YOU RATHER TIME TRAVEL TO THE LAST DAY OF ELEMENTARY SCHOOL OR THE FIRST DAY OF HIGH SCHOOL?

109

WOULD YOU RATHER GO TO THE CONCERT OF YOUR FAVORITE SINGER ALONE OR GO TO THE CONCERT OF A TERRIBLE SINGER WITH A BUNCH OF FRIENDS?

110

WOULD YOU RATHER HAVE THE ABILITY TO ONLY HEAL YOUR WOUNDS OR HEAL EVERYONE ELSE BUT YOURSELF?

111

WOULD YOU RATHER GO BACK IN TIME TO CHANGE HISTORY OR SEE THE FUTURE?

112

WOULD YOU RATHER BE FORCED TO EAT A MEAL YOU HATE OR HAVE A FRIEND CHOOSE AN UGLY OUTFIT FOR YOU TO WEAR?

113

WOULD YOU RATHER LIVE IN A HOME FULL OF SNAKES OR IN A HAUNTED MANSION?

114

WOULD YOU RATHER BE A FAMOUS CHEF OR A FAMOUS ACTOR?

115

WOULD YOU RATHER HAVE EVERY ANIMAL YOU TOUCH BECOME YOUR PET OR OWN A PET DINOSAUR?

116

WOULD YOU RATHER MOVE TO A NEW HOME AND A NEW CITY EVERY MONTH OR NEVER MOVE AT ALL?

117
WOULD YOU RATHER TRAVEL TO A NEW COUNTRY FOR A YEAR OR EXPLORE A DIFFERENT PLANET?

118
WOULD YOU RATHER COME BACK TO LIFE AS AN ANIMAL OR A GHOST?

119
WOULD YOU RATHER BE BORN HAVING NO MUSCLES IN YOUR ARMS OR NO MUSCLES IN YOUR LEGS?

120
WOULD YOU RATHER ONLY USE A SPOON OR CHOPSTICKS DURING MEALS FOR THE REST OF YOUR LIFE?

121
WOULD YOU RATHER SPONTANEOUSLY DANCE TO EVERY SONG IN PUBLIC OR HAVE TO SING EVERYTHING YOU WANT TO SAY?

122

WOULD YOU RATHER BE IN A SNOWSTORM WEARING SUMMER CLOTHES FOR AN HOUR OR IN A SCORCHING HOT DESERT WRAPPED IN A PLASTIC BAG FOR AN HOUR?

123

WOULD YOU RATHER RIDE A ROLLERCOASTER THAT IS MISSING A BUNCH OF SCREWS OR BUNGEE JUMP WITH A FRAYED ROPE?

124

WOULD YOU RATHER BRUSH YOUR TEETH WITHOUT TOOTHPASTE OR SHOWER WITHOUT SOAP FOR THE REST OF YOUR LIFE?

125

WOULD YOU RATHER SPEND YOUR WHOLE DAY IN A HAMMOCK 60 FEET FROM THE GROUND OR IN A CAVE 60 FEET BELOW GROUND?

126

WOULD YOU RATHER HAVE A PACK OF DOGS OR A TASER BE YOUR PROTECTION AGAINST A BURGLAR?

127

WOULD YOU RATHER HAVE THE ABILITY TO DISGUISE YOURSELF OR TURN INVISIBLE?

128

WOULD YOU RATHER TRAVEL TO THE MOON OR TRAVEL TO MARS?

129

WOULD YOU RATHER LIVE TO NEVER SEE SNOW OR LIVE IN A PLACE THAT IS ALWAYS SNOWY?

130

WOULD YOU RATHER BE ALLERGIC TO KITTENS OR ALWAYS GET SICK FROM EATING YOUR FAVORITE FOOD?

131

WOULD YOU RATHER HAVE SUPERHUMAN STRENGTH OR THE ABILITY TO RUN 60 MPH?

132
WOULD YOU RATHER EAT RAW FISH OR HALF-BAKED PIZZA?

133
WOULD YOU RATHER LIVE IN A HUT ON THE BEACH OR IN A TREE HOUSE IN A FOREST?

134
WOULD YOU RATHER SPEND THE WEEKEND IN A SNOW CAVE OR NEXT TO AN ACTIVE VOLCANO?

135
WOULD YOU RATHER LIVE IN A MANSION WITH NO INTERNET OR LIVE IN A SHACK WITH HIGH SPEED INTERNET?

136
WOULD YOU RATHER NOT BE ABLE TO WATCH ONLINE VIDEOS OR NOT BE ABLE TO TEXT YOUR FRIENDS FOR SIX MONTHS?

137

WOULD YOU RATHER LIVE IN A BIG MANSION IN THE MIDDLE OF NOWHERE OR LIVE IN A TINY APARTMENT WITH NO YARD IN THE MIDDLE OF THE CITY?

138

WOULD YOU RATHER BE BEAUTIFUL AND DUMB OR UNATTRACTIVE AND BRILLIANT?

139

WOULD YOU RATHER BE A FAMOUS PAINTER OR A BRILLIANT SCIENTIST?

140

WOULD YOU RATHER HAVE A HOVERBOARD OR A SURFBOARD?

141

WOULD YOU RATHER LIVE IN A WORLD THAT WAS TAKEN OVER BY ROBOTS OR ALIENS?

142

WOULD YOU RATHER HAVE YOUR LIFE BE LIKE A LIVE ACTION MOVIE OR LIKE A FUNNY CARTOON?

143

WOULD YOU RATHER NEVER WAIT IN LINE AGAIN OR NEVER GET A HEAD COLD AGAIN?

144

WOULD YOU RATHER NEVER BE ABLE TO WEAR PANTS OR NEVER BE ABLE TO WEAR SHOES?

145

WOULD YOU RATHER SPEND MOST OF YOUR LIFE IN A PLANE OR IN A SUBMARINE?

146

WOULD YOU RATHER BE THE PITCHER FOR A FAMOUS BASEBALL TEAM OR THE CHEERLEADER FOR A FAMOUS FOOTBALL TEAM?

147

WOULD YOU RATHER TRIP WHILE RUNNING IN A STATE TRACK MEET OR FORGET A SPEECH IN FRONT OF 1,000 PEOPLE.

148

WOULD YOU RATHER NEVER HAVE TO DO LAUNDRY AGAIN OR NEVER DO DISHES AGAIN?

149

WOULD YOU RATHER WEAR THE SAME UNIFORM EVERY SINGLE DAY OR WEAR MATCHING SWEATERS WITH YOUR PARENTS?

150

WOULD YOU RATHER NEVER LOSE YOUR PHONE AGAIN OR NEVER LOSE YOUR WALLET AGAIN?

151

WOULD YOU RATHER HAVE FIFTEEN KIDS OR HAVE NO KIDS FOR YOUR ENTIRE LIFE?

152

WOULD YOU RATHER FIND A SUITCASE WITH EIGHT MILLION DOLLARS OR A SOULMATE?

153

WOULD YOU RATHER STAY AS A CHILD OR AS AN ADULT FOR THE REST OF YOUR LIFE?

154

WOULD YOU RATHER BE CHASED BY VICIOUS DOGS OR SCARY CLOWNS?

155

WOULD YOU RATHER BE CONSTANTLY HUNGRY OR EXTREMELY DEHYDRATED?

156

WOULD YOU RATHER HAVE A PHONE WITH UNLIMITED BATTERY LIFE OR A CAR WITH UNLIMITED GAS?

157

WOULD YOU RATHER BE ATTACKED BY A SHARK OR A BEAR?

158

WOULD YOU RATHER FEED A SNAKE OR A SHARK BY HAND?

159

WOULD YOU RATHER WORK TWENTY HOURS PER DAY, TWO DAYS A WEEK OR WORK SIX HOURS PER DAY, SEVEN DAYS A WEEK?

160

WOULD YOU RATHER RUIN A FRIEND'S WEDDING OR FUNERAL?

161

WOULD YOU RATHER BE WITHOUT A SHOWER FOR A MONTH OR WITHOUT YOUR PHONE FOR A MONTH?

162

WOULD YOU RATHER HAVE MOVIES OR MUSIC AS YOUR ONLY ENTERTAINMENT FOR THE REST OF YOUR LIFE?

163

WOULD YOU RATHER RECEIVE CASH OR GIFTS FOR CHRISTMAS?

164

WOULD YOU RATHER READ MINDS OR BE ABLE TO COMMUNICATE WITH PEOPLE IN THEIR DREAMS?

165

WOULD YOU RATHER HAVE A CURE FOR DISEASES OR END WORLD HUNGER?

166

WOULD YOU RATHER SPEND A WEEKEND IN A CITY OF YOUR CHOICE AT A 5-STAR HOTEL OR GO CAMPING IN THE GREAT OUTDOORS?

167

WOULD YOU RATHER SEE A DRAGON IN REAL LIFE OR A SEA MONSTER IN REAL LIFE?

168

WOULD YOU RATHER FIGHT FOR SURVIVAL IN A ZOMBIE APOCALYPSE OR IN AN ALIEN INVASION?

169

WOULD YOU RATHER BE STUCK ON AN ISLAND BY YOURSELF OR LOST ON A MOUNTAIN BY YOURSELF?

170

WOULD YOU RATHER WIN THE LOTTERY OR BE ABLE TO FLY?

171

WOULD YOU RATHER SIT THROUGH A MOVIE THEATRE FOR 24 HOURS OR A MUSICAL CONCERT FOR 24 HOURS?

172

WOULD YOU RATHER HAVE A JOB WHERE YOU WORK INDOORS ALL THE TIME OR WORK OUTDOORS ALL THE TIME, RAIN OR SHINE?

173

WOULD YOU RATHER STAY IN A HAUNTED MANSION TWO DAYS OR BE STUCK IN AN ELEVATOR FOR TWO DAYS?

174

WOULD YOU RATHER BUILD YOUR OWN HOUSE OR BUILD YOUR OWN CAR?

175

WOULD YOU RATHER BE TRAPPED UPSIDE DOWN IN A ROLLER COASTER FOR 20 MINUTES OR IN AN OUTHOUSE FOR AN HOUR?

176

WOULD YOU RATHER SPEND THE DAY WITH YOUR IDOL OR WITH YOUR SOULMATE?

177

WOULD YOU RATHER BUILD ALL OF YOUR OWN FURNITURE OR SEW ALL OF YOUR OWN CLOTHES?

178

WOULD YOU RATHER WORK AT A JOB YOU HATE BUT THAT PAYS WELL OR WORK AT A JOB THAT YOU LOVE THAT PAYS VERY LITTLE.

179

WOULD YOU RATHER BE IN A SWIMSUIT OR IN YOUR PAJAMAS ALL DAY?

180

WOULD YOU RATHER GO WITHOUT JUNK FOOD OR WITHOUT INTERNET FOR THE REST OF YOUR LIFE?

181

WOULD YOU RATHER SPEND A DAY AT THE BEACH OR AT THE MALL?

182

WOULD YOU RATHER HAVE THE ABILITY TO BE AN EXPERT AT COOKING FOOD FROM AROUND THE WORLD OR BE FLUENT IN ALL LANGUAGES?

183

WOULD YOU RATHER LOSE YOUR OWN MEMORY OR YOUR FRIENDS AND FAMILY FORGET WHO YOU ARE?

184

WOULD YOU RATHER OWN A FARM OR A MANSION?

185

WOULD YOU RATHER BE ABLE TO FLY THROUGH SPACE WITHOUT NEEDING A SPACE SUIT OR BREATH UNDERWATER FOR AS LONG AS YOU WANT?

186

WOULD YOU RATHER ENTER A DANCE-OFF OR A KARAOKE CONTEST?

187

WOULD YOU RATHER HAVE PEOPLE BEFRIEND YOU FOR YOUR GOOD LOOKS OR INTELLIGENCE?

188

WOULD YOU RATHER GIVE UP YOUR FAVORITE ICE CREAM OR FAVORITE BEVERAGE FOR THE REST OF YOUR LIFE?

189

WOULD YOU RATHER CHANGE YOUR HEIGHT OR YOUR BODY SHAPE?

190

WOULD YOU RATHER HAVE YOUR FRIENDS KNOW OF YOUR MOST EMBARRASSING MOMENTS OR GIVE A SPEECH IN FRONT OF A PACKED AUDITORIUM?

191

WOULD YOU RATHER HAVE HEAT RESISTANCE OR COLD RESISTANCE?

192

WOULD YOU RATHER RUN FOR PRESIDENT OR HELP SOMEONE ELSE RUN FOR PRESIDENT?

193

WOULD YOU RATHER GET TO LIVE IN YOUR FAVORITE MOVIE OR TOUR WITH YOUR FAVORITE BAND?

194

WOULD YOU RATHER GET 2 HOURS OF SLEEP EVERY NIGHT OR USE THE INTERNET FOR ONLY TEN MINUTES EACH DAY?

195

WOULD YOU RATHER LOSE YOUR MEMORY BUT STILL HAVE THE ABILITY TO SPEAK AND WRITE OR KEEP YOUR MEMORY BUT NEVER BE ABLE TO SPEAK OR WRITE AGAIN?

196

WOULD YOU RATHER STAND IN A LONG LINE FOR THREE HOURS OR SIT THROUGH TRAFFIC FOR THREE HOURS?

197

WOULD YOU RATHER GIVE UP BREAD OR DAIRY PRODUCTS FOREVER?

198

WOULD YOU RATHER MARRY A RICH, UNHAPPY PERSON OR A POOR, HAPPY PERSON?

199

WOULD YOU RATHER HAVE A SCORPION OR A TARANTULA AS A PET?

200

WOULD YOU RATHER LOOK UNATTRACTIVE BUT SMELL GOOD OR HAVE GOOD LOOKS BUT SMELL BAD?

201

WOULD YOU RATHER LIE ABOUT YOUR PAST OR LIE ABOUT YOUR AGE?

202

WOULD YOU RATHER HAVE A BIG HEAD WITH A SMALL BODY OR A BIG BODY WITH A SMALL HEAD?

203

WOULD YOU RATHER WAKE UP IN THE MORNING AS A MONKEY OR AS A DONKEY?

204

WOULD YOU RATHER STAY YOUR WHOLE LIFE AS A CHILD AND CONTINUE TO LIVE WITH YOUR PARENTS OR GROW UP OVERNIGHT AND BE OUT ON YOUR OWN?

205

WOULD YOU RATHER BE UNABLE TO STOP TALKING TO STUFFED ANIMALS OR BE UNABLE TO DANCE IN FRONT OF A WINDOW EVERY TIME YOU WALK BY?

206

WOULD YOU RATHER HAVE $1 MILLION NOW OR HAVE $200 EVERY DAY FOR THE REST OF YOUR LIFE?

207

WOULD YOU RATHER HAVE MANY BEST FRIENDS OR ONE ROMANTIC PARTNER?

208

WOULD YOU RATHER DEFEND YOURSELF AGAINST 100 CHICKENS OR A TEN-FOOT DUCK?

209

WOULD YOU RATHER HAVE THE ABILITY GET SKINNIER OR SMARTER?

210

WOULD YOU RATHER HAVE A BEAR CHASE YOU FOR FIVE MINUTES OR RIDE A BULL FOR FIVE MINUTES?

211

WOULD YOU RATHER HAVE TO GO TO THE BATHROOM IN A LITTER BOX OR IN YOUR FRONT YARD?

212

WOULD YOU RATHER RECEIVE 100 DOLLARS OR 100 LOTTERY TICKETS?

213

WOULD YOU RATHER HAVE A HUGE NOSE WITH MINIATURE EARS OR A MINIATURE NOSE WITH HUGE EARS?

214

WOULD YOU RATHER BE BORN WITHOUT TOENAILS AND FINGERNAILS OR A BELLY BUTTON THAT SHOUTS AT PEOPLE AS YOU WALK BY?

215

WOULD YOU RATHER LOSE YOUR EYESIGHT BUT BE ABLE TO HEAR REALLY WELL OR BE ABLE TO SEE BUT NOT HEAR AT ALL?

216

WOULD YOU RATHER ENTER A BOXING MATCH WITH NO GLOVES OR A SOCCER GAME WITH NO SHOES?

217

WOULD YOU RATHER BE FORCED TO BE IN A TALENT SHOW OR IN A RUNNING RACE?

218

WOULD YOU RATHER CARRY FOUR CHICKENS FOR EIGHT HOURS OR A MONKEY ON YOUR BACK FOR 16 HOURS?

219

WOULD YOU RATHER HAVE LIVE IN A HOUSEBOAT OR IN AN APARTMENT IN A BUSY CITY?

220

WOULD YOU RATHER TAKE A REALLY COLD SHOWER FOR 30 MINUTES OR SIT IN A SUPER HOT STEAM ROOM FOR ONE HOUR?

221

WOULD YOU RATHER GIVE UP YOUR WALLET OR GIVE UP YOUR CLOTHES WHEN GETTING ROBBED?

222

WOULD YOU RATHER BE A GIANT BUNNY OR A TINY T-REX?

223

WOULD YOU RATHER HAVE A PET DINOSAUR THAT GOES ON A RAMPAGE ACROSS THE CITY OR BE TURNED INTO A DINOSAUR?

224

WOULD YOU RATHER HAVE THREE WISHES GRANTED TODAY OR ONE WISH GRANTED EVERY YEAR?

225

WOULD YOU RATHER BE SHOVED INTO A LOCKER OR GET YOUR HEAD STUCK IN A BUCKET?

226

WOULD YOU RATHER HAVE LONG FINGERS OR A LONG NECK?

227

WOULD YOU RATHER BE CAUGHT IN A TORNADO OR AN EARTHQUAKE?

228

WOULD YOU RATHER HAVE IT RAIN HONEY OR COCONUTS?

229

WOULD YOU RATHER SIT IN A THUNDERSTORM OR A SNOWSTORM?

230

WOULD YOU RATHER HAVE NO ARMS OR NO LEGS?

231

WOULD YOU RATHER HAVE NO NOSE OR NO NECK?

232

WOULD YOU RATHER GET GORED BY A BULL IN THE SHOULDER OR KICKED BY A HORSE IN THE BACK?

233

WOULD YOU RATHER HAVE THE ABILITY TO CONTROL OTHER PEOPLE'S WORDS OR CONTROL PEOPLE'S THOUGHTS?

234

WOULD YOU RATHER GET TURNED INTO A DOG THAT TALKS OR REMAIN HUMAN BUT BE ONLY ABLE TO BARK FOR THE REST OF YOUR LIFE?

235

WOULD YOU RATHER WEAR A SWIMSUIT AT YOUR JOB FOR THE ENTIRE SHIFT OR WEAR A BUSINESS SUIT AT A BEACH FOR THE DAY?

236

WOULD YOU RATHER EAT A CAN OF CHICKEN-FLAVORED CAT FOOD OR A SMALL JAR OF MASHED BROCCOLI BABY FOOD FOR BREAKFAST?

237

WOULD YOU RATHER GET ATTACKED BY GRIZZLY BEAR OR A MOUNTAIN LION?

238

WOULD YOU RATHER RUN AROUND A PARK WITH NO CLOTHES ON FOR 20 MINUTES OR GO TO A RESTAURANT WITH A DIAPER ON?

239
WOULD YOU RATHER HAVE A NECK LIKE A GIRAFFE OR EARS LIKE AN ELEPHANT?

240
WOULD YOU RATHER HAVE ARMS LIKE A GORILLA OR LEGS LIKE A CHEETAH?

241
WOULD YOU RATHER HAVE YOUR EYEBROWS AND LASHES SHAVED OR YOUR HEAD SHAVED?

242
WOULD YOU RATHER HAVE HANDS FOR FEET OR FEET FOR HANDS?

243
WOULD YOU RATHER READ PEOPLE'S MINDS OR CONTROL THEIR MINDS?

244
WOULD YOU RATHER LICK THE INSIDE OF A TOILET OR WASH YOUR HAIR WITH TOILET WATER?

245

WOULD YOU RATHER LIVE IN A CONVENT OR BECOME A MONK?

246

WOULD YOU RATHER HAVE A DOG FACE OR A DOG BODY?

247

WOULD YOU RATHER EAT CHOCOLATE-COVERED CHICKEN OR CHICKEN-FLAVORED CHOCOLATE?

248

WOULD YOU RATHER HAVE A CLOSET FULL OF GREEN CLOTHES OR RED CLOTHES?

249

WOULD YOU RATHER HAVE 4 ARMS OR 1 FINGER ON EACH HAND?

250

WOULD YOU RATHER BE CHASED BY AN ARMY OF PORCUPINES OR WAKE UP IN BED WITH A BEAR IN FRONT OF YOU?

251

WOULD YOU SAY "UM" AFTER EVERY OTHER WORD OR SNEEZE EVERYTIME YOU SAY "THE"

252

WOULD YOU RATHER BEFRIEND A GROUP OF LEPRECHAUNS OR FIND GOLD AT THE END OF A RAINBOW?

253

WOULD YOU RATHER HAVE THE WORLD TAKEN OVER BY BUNNIES OR KITTENS?

254

WOULD YOU RATHER HAVE THE ABILITY TO TRANSFORM INTO A DIFFERENT PERSON OR A DIFFERENT ANIMAL?

255

WOULD YOU RATHER HAVE THE ABILITY TO PLAY EVERY MUSICAL INSTRUMENT OR BE A MASTER AT EVERY SPORT?

256

WOULD YOU RATHER HAVE WINGS OR WEAR A TURTLE SHELL FOR THE REST OF YOUR LIFE?

257

WOULD YOU RATHER SIT IN A CAVE FULL OF BATS FOR ONE HOUR OR GO SHARK-CAGE DIVING FOR 15 MINUTES?

258

WOULD YOU RATHER GIVE UP YOUR INTERNET OR EAT THE SAME MEAL FOR BREAKFAST, LUNCH, AND DINNER FOR THE REST OF YOUR LIFE?

259

WOULD YOU RATHER LOSE ALL OF YOUR FRIENDSHIPS THROUGHOUT YOUR LIFE OR GIVE UP ALL OF THE MONEY YOU HAVE SAVED UP?

260

WOULD YOU RATHER GO TO A BEACH WITHOUT SUNSCREEN FOR THE ENTIRE DAY OR HIKE UP A MOUNTAIN IN THE WINTER WITH NO JACKET?

261

WOULD YOU RATHER BE JUDGED FOR YOUR HONESTY OR BE PRAISED FOR A LIE?

262

WOULD YOU RATHER WAKE UP TO YOUR HOUSE BURNING, AND EVEN THOUGH YOU ESCAPE, NOTHING IS LEFT BUT ASHES OR WAKE UP IN THE WOODS AND NOT KNOW WHO YOU ARE OR WHERE YOUR HOME IS?

263

WOULD YOU RATHER HAVE THE ABILITY TO CONTROL TIME OR THE ABILITY TO CONTROL THE WEATHER?

264

WOULD YOU RATHER HAVE YOUR CHOICES BE MADE BY YOUR FRIENDS OR YOUR PARENTS?

265

WOULD YOU RATHER ADOPT A LION OR A BEAR?

266

WOULD YOU RATHER HAVE BEEN WITH THE WRIGHT BROTHERS WHEN THEY TOOK THEIR FIRST FLIGHT OR WITH THOMAS EDISON AS HE REALIZED THE SUCCESS OF THE ELECTRIC LIGHTBULB?

267

WOULD YOU RATHER GO BACK IN TIME TO MEET ELVIS OR THE BEATLES?

268

WOULD YOU RATHER GO BACK IN TIME TO MEET MUHAMMAD ALI OR JOAN OF ARC?

269

WOULD YOU RATHER HAVE BAD EYESIGHT OR HEARING LOSS FOR THE REST OF YOUR LIFE?

270

WOULD YOU RATHER BE IGNORED OR GET YELLED AT?

271

WOULD YOU RATHER BE SURROUNDED BY PEOPLE WHO ARE HYPER AND TALK NONSTOP OR BY PEOPLE WHO COMPLAIN ALL THE TIME?

272

WOULD YOU RATHER HEAR A HURTFUL TRUTH OR TELL A COMFORTING LIE?

273

WOULD YOU RATHER BE A HARD WORKER OR HAVE A LOT OF LUCK?

274

WOULD YOU RATHER GO BACK IN TIME TO TRAVEL WITH LEWIS AND CLARK OR GO FORWARD IN TIME TO WITNESS THE INVENTION OF AN AQUATIC TREADMILL?

275

WOULD YOU RATHER RIDE A DINOSAUR OR A KANGAROO?

276

WOULD YOU RATHER FORGET HOW TO READ OR HOW TO WRITE?

277

WOULD YOU RATHER LOSE ALL YOUR MONEY BUT SAVE A LIFE OR KEEP ALL YOUR MONEY AND WATCH SOMEONE DIE?

278

WOULD YOU RATHER GO CAMPING WITHOUT A TENT OR WITHOUT A SLEEPING BAG?

279

WOULD YOU RATHER FORGET FOOD OR SHELTER WHEN BACKPACKING FOR 3 NIGHTS?

280

WOULD YOU RATHER GO THROUGH THREE MONTHS WITHOUT BRUSHING YOUR HAIR OR WITHOUT CUTTING YOUR NAILS?

281

WOULD YOU RATHER ACTORS GET REPLACED BY ROBOTS OR HAVE IT BE NORMAL FOR EVERY HOUSHOLD TO HAVE A ROBOT LIVE WITH THEM?

282

WOULD YOU RATHER GO THROUGH AN ENTIRE WINTER WITHOUT A HEATER OR AN ENTIRE SUMMER WITHOUT AIR CONDITIONING?

283

WOULD YOU RATHER GET A HUG FROM SOMEONE WHO SMELLS OR GET LICKED BY A STRANGER?

284

WOULD YOU RATHER DATE SOMEONE YOU DON'T LIKE OR DATE YOUR CRUSH WHO DOESN'T REALLY LIKE YOU?

285

WOULD YOU RATHER BE A A NERDY HIGH SCHOOL STUDENT OR 40-YEARS-OLD FOR THE REST OF YOUR LIFE?

286

WOULD YOU RATHER GET BIT BY A ZOMBIE OR A VAMPIRE?

287

WOULD YOU RATHER TRANSFORM INTO A WOLF OR A BAT?

288

WOULD YOU RATHER GET BIT BY TEN MOSQUITOS OR STUNG BY ONE BEE?

289

WOULD YOU RATHER SLEEP ON A TRAMPOLINE OR LIVE IN A BOUNCE HOUSE FOR ONE MONTH?

290

WOULD YOU RATHER HAVE YOUR PHONE DESTROYED OR ALL OF YOUR PHOTOS AND TEXTS LEAKED TO THE PUBLIC?

291

WOULD YOU RATHER GIVE A BABY A BATH OR 3 CATS A BATH?

292

WOULD YOU RATHER WEAR THE SAME THING AS YOUR DAD EVERYDAY OR HAVE THE SAME HAIRSTYLE AS YOUR DAD?

293

WOULD YOU RATHER GO BACK IN TIME TO TOUR WITH QUEEN OR THE ROLLING STONES?

294

WOULD YOU RATHER HURT YOUR FRIEND'S FEELINGS BY BEING HONEST OR KEEP YOUR FAMILY HAPPY BY LYING?

295
WOULD YOU RATHER WATCH YOUR FRIEND GET
ATTACKED BY WOLVES OR GET ATTACKED YOURSELF?

296
WOULD YOU RATHER LOSE ALL OF YOUR MONEY OR
LOSE ALL OF YOUR SENTIMENTAL VALUABLES?

297
WOULD YOU RATHER LIVE IN A CASTLE OR A PYRAMID
FOR A YEAR?

298
WOULD YOU RATHER BE THE ONLY HUMAN IN THE WORLD
OR GO THROUGH A ZOMBIE OUTBREAK WITH A CHANCE
OF SURVIVORS?

299
WOULD YOU RATHER HAVE ALL OF YOUR CLOTHES
STOLEN OR ALL OF YOUR VALUABLES SMASHED?

300

WOULD YOU RATHER GO THROUGH THREE DAYS WITHOUT EATING OR 24 HOURS WITHOUT FLUID?

301

WOULD YOU RATHER LIVE IN A CAR AT THE TOP OF A MOUNTAIN OR IN A BOAT IN THE MIDDLE OF THE OCEAN FOR ONE MONTH?

302

WOULD YOU RATHER DROP YOUR PHONE IN THE OCEAN OR HAVE YOUR PHONE RUN OVER BY A CAR?

303

WOULD YOU RATHER GIVE UP FAST FOOD OR GIVE UP BEVERAGES?

304

WOULD YOU RATHER LICK A FRIEND'S FEET OR LICK A FRIEND'S ARMPIT?

305

WOULD YOU RATHER SIT THROUGH A TEN-HOUR MOVIE
OR BE TRAPPED IN AN EMPTY ROOM FOR TEN HOURS?

306

WOULD YOU RATHER EAT NOTHING BUT RAW EGGS FOR
24 HOURS OR EAT RAW CHICKEN?

307

WOULD YOU RATHER RUB A FRIEND'S SWEATY BELLY OR
MASSAGE A FRIEND'S DIRTY FEET?

308

WOULD YOU RATHER HAVE YOUR BODY COVERED IN
FEATHERS OR SCALES?

309

WOULD YOU RATHER HAVE RATS OR COCKROACHES
INVADE YOUR HOME?

310

WOULD YOU RATHER PAINT YOUR WALLS WITH A TOOTHBRUSH OR BRUSH YOUR TEETH WITH A PAINTBRUSH?

311

WOULD YOU RATHER HAVE THE ABILITY TO SILENCE SOMEONE OR CONTROL THEIR SPEAKING?

312

WOULD YOU RATHER HAVE A FRIEND LICK YOUR ARMPITS OR YOUR FEET?

313

WOULD YOU RATHER OWN YOUR OWN COFFEE SHOP OR RESTAURANT?

314

WOULD YOU RATHER GET STUCK IN A MOSH PIT OR ENTER A SKATEBOARD CONTEST?

315

WOULD YOU RATHER GET PINCHED 100 TIMES A DAY OR TICKLED FOR ONE MINUTE, TWENTY TIMES A DAY?

316

WOULD YOU RATHER HAVE HAIRY KNUCKELS OR A HAIRY NECK?

317

WOULD YOU RATHER BE BANNED FROM EVER EATING AT RESTAURANTS OR BANNED FROM EVER SEEING A MOVIE IN A THEATRE AGAIN?

318

WOULD YOU RATHER BE 30 POUNDS OVERWEIGHT OR BE 30 POUNDS UNDERWEIGHT?

319

WOULD YOU RATHER HAVE AN EVIL TWIN OR AN EVIL CHILD?

320

WOULD YOU RATHER BE A PIG FARMER OR AN ALASKAN LONGSHOREMAN?

321

WOULD YOU RATHER BE A FOOTBALL OR A SOCCER BALL?

322

WOULD YOU RATHER BE SWEPT AWAY BY BALLOONS OR SQUISHED OUT OF YOUR ROOM BY TOO MANY STUFFED ANIMALS?

323

WOULD YOU RATHER HAVE PIE WITH WHIPPED CREAM OR WITH ICE CREAM?

324

WOULD YOU RATHER HAVE AN INSATIABLE ITCH OR LOSE THE FEELING IN YOUR FINGERTIPS?

325

WOULD YOU RATHER BE CHASED BY CLOWNS OR CHASE A GROUP OF SCHOOL CHILDREN DRESSED AS CLOWNS?

326

WOULD YOU RATHER LOSE THE ABILITY TO USE YOUR CREDIT OR DEBIT CARD OR LOSE THE ABILITY TO USE CASH?

327

WOULD YOU RATHER ONLY PAY WITH PENNIES OR CUT YOUR NEIGHBORHOOD'S GRASS WITH SCISSORS EVERY MONTH?

328

WOULD YOU RATHER HAVE THE ABILITY TO KNOW EVERYONE'S SECRETS OR THE ABILITY TO MAKE PEOPLE PAY FOR YOUR FOOD?

329

WOULD YOU RATHER HAVE ENDLESS ENERGY BUT NEED TO SLEEP 15 HOURS A DAY OR BE TIRED ALL TIME AND ONLY ABLE TO SLEEP FOUR HOURS A DAY?

330

WOULD YOU RATHER LIVE WITH AN ANNOYING FRIEND OR WITH YOUR PARENTS FOR THE REST OF YOUR LIFE?

331

WOULD YOU RATHER HAVE CHRISTMAS TWICE A YEAR OR HALLOWEEN FIVE TIMES A YEAR?

332

WOULD YOU RATHER LOSE YOUR FRIENDSHIP OVER A BOARD GAME OR LOSE EVERY TIME?

333

WOULD YOU RATHER GET ARRESTED FOR ROBBING A CANDY STORE OR FOR STEALING A PUPPY?

334

WOULD YOU RATHER HAVE ALIENS COME TO EARTH OR TALKING ANIMALS EXIST?

335

WOULD YOU RATHER BECOME AN ANIMAL OF YOUR CHOICE OR HAVE ALL OF YOUR FRIENDS TURN INTO KITTENS?

336

WOULD YOU RATHER USE SOMEONE ELSES TOOTHBRUSH OR TAKE A SHOWER WITH A PET?

337

WOULD YOU RATHER BE FORCED TO WATCH YOUR FRIEND FLOSS THEIR TEETH OR FORCE THEM TO WATCH YOU FLOSS YOUR TEETH?

338

WOULD YOU RATHER BRUSH YOUR FRIEND'S TEETH EVERY MORNING OR COOK BREAKFAST FOR YOUR FRIEND EVERY MORNING?

339

WOULD YOU RATHER TRANSFORM INTO AN INSECT OF YOUR CHOICE OR A FISH OF YOUR CHOICE?

340
WOULD YOU RATHER BE FORCED TO READ EVERY BOOK EVER WRITTEN OR WATCH EVERY MOVIE EVER MADE?

341
WOULD YOU RATHER JUMP OVER A RAGING CREEK OR WALK A MILE UPHILL TO GO AROUND IT?

342
WOULD YOU RATHER DRAW EVERYTHING YOU SEE PERFECTLY OR SING EVERY SONG YOU LISTENED TO BEAUTIFULLY?

343
WOULD YOU RATHER THROW A PIE AT A STRANGER'S FACE OR TELL A STRANGER THEY ARE THE MOST BEAUTIFUL PERSON YOU HAVE EVER SEEN?

344
WOULD YOU RATHER BE RECORDED GETTING SPANKED 20 TIMES OR RECORDED GETTING TICKLED FOR ONE MINUTE?

345

WOULD YOU RATHER PUT YOUR HAND ON A MOUSETRAP OR DIP YOUR FACE IN SALSA?

346

WOULD YOU RATHER HAVE A TAIL OR WEBBED FEET?

347

WOULD YOU RATHER GET IN A FIGHT WITH A KANGAROO OR 30 ROOSTERS?

348

WOULD YOU RATHER LOOK JUST LIKE YOUR NEIGHBOR OR HAVE EVERYONE IN THE WHOLE WORLD LOOK LIKE YOU?

349

WOULD YOU RATHER LOOK JUST LIKE YOUR FRIEND OR HAVE A FRIEND LOOK EXACTLY LIKE YOU?

350

WOULD YOU RATHER HAVE 50 FISH THROWN AT YOU AND GET PAID $500 OR PAY $50 TO NOT HAVE 50 FISH THROWN AT YOU?

351

WOULD YOU RATHER HAVE WEATHER LITERALLY RAIN CATS OR LITERALLY RAIN DOGS?

352

WOULD YOU RATHER HAVE A LEMON-SHAPED HEAD OR A HEAD AS HEAVY AS A BOWLING BALL?

353

WOULD YOU RATHER BE A TOILET OR A BAR OF SOAP?

354

WOULD YOU RATHER HAVE ANTLERS OR A LION'S MANE?

355

WOULD YOU RATHER BE YOUR FAVORITE COMIC OR BOOK CHARACTER OR BE A MOVIE STAR IN YOUR FAVORITE MOVIE?

356

WOULD YOU RATHER HAVE A CITY DESTROYED BY A GIANT SPIDER OR A GIANT SNAKE?

357

WOULD YOU RATHER GET STOMPED ON OR BUG SPRAYED IF YOU WERE AN INSECT?

358

WOULD YOU RATHER MOVE TO AN ISLAND OR LIVE IN A SKYSCRAPER WITH A ROOFTOP POOL?

359

WOULD YOU RATHER LEARN TO PILOT A PLANE OR NAVIGATE A SUBMARINE?

360

WOULD YOU RATHER EAT A WHOLE STICK OF BUTTER OR 5 RAW EGGS?

361

WOULD YOU RATHER BUILD YOUR OWN HOUSE WITH POPSICLE STICKS OR CLAY?

362

WOULD YOU RATHER SHAVE PEOPLE'S ARMPIT AS A FULL TIME JOB OR CLEAN TOENAILS AS A FULL TIME JOB?

363

WOULD YOU RATHER STAY YOUNG AND POOR FOR THE REST OF YOUR LIFE OR GROW OLD WITH ONE MILLION DOLLARS BUT ONLY HAVE TEN YEARS LEFT TO LIVE?

364

WOULD YOU RATHER HAVE AN EXPENSIVE HOUSE WITH A CAR IN POOR CONDITION OR HAVE AN EXPENSIVE CAR BUT LIVE IN A SHACK?

365

WOULD YOU RATHER COME BACK TO LIFE AS A PLANT OR A ROCK?

366

WOULD YOU RATHER BE AN ASTRONAUT OR A CRUISE DIRECTOR?

367

WOULD YOU RATHER MELT LIKE ICE CREAM OR GROW MOLD LIKE BREAD?

368

WOULD YOU RATHER SPEND FIVE HOURS IN A HOT TUB OR IN A COLD POOL?

369

WOULD YOU RATHER HAVE TIGER STRIPES OR FURRY ARMS?

370

WOULD YOU RATHER BE A FULL-TIME STUDENT WITH NO RESPONSIBILITIES AT ALL OR HAVE A GREAT JOB AND BE REALLY BUSY?

371

WOULD YOU RATHER HAVE AN EXTRA EYE OR AN EXTRA ARM?

372

WOULD YOU RATHER SWIM 100 METERS THROUGH SOUR MILK OR 100 METERS THROUGH A SWAMP?

373

WOULD YOU RATHER SKIP TEN YEARS INTO THE FUTURE OR GO TEN YEARS BACK IN TIME?

373

WOULD YOU RATHER EXPERIENCE THE TRIASSIC PERIOD OR THE MEDIEVAL AGES?

374

WOULD YOU RATHER HAVE MET PICASSO OR GEORGE WASHINGTON?

375

WOULD YOU RATHER BE BORN WITHOUT LEGS OR WITHOUT ARMS?

376

WOULD YOU RATHER KNOW WHEN YOU WILL DIE OR WHEN YOUR LOVED ONES WILL DIE?

377

WOULD YOU RATHER TRAVEL TO ITALY TO EAT PIZZA OR TRAVEL TO JAPAN TO EAT SUSHI?

378

WOULD YOU RATHER ONLY SEE THE COLOR RED OR ONLY SEE THE COLOR BLUE FOR THE REST OF YOUR LIFE?

379

WOULD YOU RATHER ONLY DRINK COFFEE OR ONLY DRINK TEA FOR THE REST OF YOUR LIFE?

380

WOULD YOU RATHER BE A PIRATE OR A VIKING?

381

WOULD YOU RATHER FIGHT A SUMO WRESTLER OR A PROFESSIONAL BOXER?

382

WOULD YOU RATHER BE ABLE TO READ YOUR DOG'S MIND OR YOUR PARTNER'S MIND?

383

WOULD YOU RATHER WIN AN UNLIMITED SHOPPING SPREE OR HELP MAKE A CLEAN WATER WELL FOR A GROUP OF PEOPLE IN A 3RD-WORLD COUNTRY?

384

WOULD YOU RATHER WEAR HIGH HEELS OR RUBBER BOOTS FOR THE REST OF YOUR LIFE?

385

WOULD YOU RATHER SAVE YOUR BEST FRIEND OR SAVE 10,000 PEOPLE YOU DON'T KNOW?

386

WOULD YOU RATHER STICK YOUR TONGUE ON A COLD POST OR PICK UP A HOT PAN WITHOUT AN OVEN MITT?

387

WOULD YOU RATHER HAVE THE ABILITY TO KNOW PEOPLE'S SECRETS BY SMELLING THEIR BREATH OR THE ABILITY TO BECOME GENIUS SMART FOR ONE MINUTE EVERY TIME YOU BURP?

388

WOULD YOU RATHER LOSE ALL OF YOUR TEETH OR LOSE ALL OF YOUR HAIR FOREVER?

389

WOULD YOU RATHER HAVE A GOOD DREAM AND NEVER WAKE UP FOR THE REST OF YOUR LIFE OR WAKE UP AND HAVE YOUR NIGHTMARES BECOME A REALITY?

390

WOULD YOU RATHER GIVE UP WEARING CLEAN CLOTHES FOR TEN YEARS OR GIVE UP SLEEPING ON A COMFORTABLE BED FOR TEN YEARS?

391

WOULD YOU RATHER GIVE A CREEPY STRANGER A RIDE OR BE STRANDED WITH NO WAY TO GET TO WHERE YOU ARE GOING?

392

WOULD YOU RATHER HAVE A UNICORN HORN OR ZEBRA STRIPES?

393

WOULD YOU RATHER HAVE YOUR GRANDMA'S HAIRSTYLE OR YOUR GRANDPA'S CLOTHES?

394

WOULD YOU RATHER BE A FAMOUS JAZZ MUSICIAN OR BE ABLE TO MEET YOUR FAVORITE MUSICIAN?

395

WOULD YOU RATHER EAT A RAW ONION OR A HABANERO PEPPER EVERY NIGHT AT DINNER?

396

WOULD YOU RATHER GIVE UP SUGAR OR COFFEE?

397

WOULD YOU RATHER LIVE IN A SHACK IN HAWAII OR A MANSION IN THE ANTARCTIC?

398

WOULD YOU RATHER WIN A MILLION DOLLARS OR LIVE 3 TIMES AS LONG?

400

WOULD YOU RATHER EXPLORE THE JUNGLE FOR A WEEK OR PLAY VIDEO GAMES ALL DAY LONG FOR A MONTH?

401

WOULD YOU RATHER HAVE A BIRD APPEAR ON YOUR SHOULDER AND CHIRP EVERY TIME YOU FORGET SOMEONE'S NAME OR A FERRET JUMP OUT OF YOUR POCKET EVERYTIME YOU SAY "UM"?

402

WOULD YOU RATHER FALL ASLEEP AN HOUR BEFORE YOUR BEDTIME EVERY NIGHT OR BE WIDE AWAKE EVERY MORNING AN HOUR BEFORE YOUR ALARM GOES OFF?

403

WOULD YOU RATHER SOMEONE GIVE YOU A YACHT OR HAVE THE KNOW HOW AND RESOURCES TO BUILD ONE?

404

WOULD YOU RATHER EAT LIVE A YEAR IN AN IGLOO OR A HOUSEBOAT ON A CANAL?

BONUS QUESTIONS!

FROM THE GROSS & CRAZY EDITION
NOW AVAILABLE ON AMAZON!

DO YOU HAVE WHAT IT TAKES? CAN YOU ANSWER
THE MOST DIFFICULT, GROSS, AND DOWNRIGHT
CRAZY WOULD YOU RATHER QUESTIONS?!

THEN GO RIGHT AHEAD...
BE OUR GUEST!

405
WOULD YOU RATHER PLAY IN A MUD PIT FILLED WITH
WORMS AND SLUGS OR PLAY IN A BATH OF ROTTING FISH?

406

WOULD YOU RATHER SWIM IN A RIVER FILLED WITH PIRANHAS OR WADE WAIST DEEP IN WATER WITH ONE SHARK?

407

WOULD YOU RATHER DRINK A GLASS OF SWEAT OR STICK YOUR HAND IN A JAR OF SNOT?

408

WOULD YOU RATHER HAVE TO DO 25 PULL-UPS ON A BAR SUSPENDED 15 FEET ABOVE ROCKY GROUND OR HAVE TO DO 75 PUSH-UPS OVER A GAP BETWEEN TWO CLIFFS?

409

WOULD YOU RATHER SWEAT UNCONTROLLABLY OR SMELL LIKE TUNA FISH ALL DAY LONG?

410

WOULD YOU RATHER HAVE SARDINES OR RAW EGGS BE THROWN AT YOU EVERY TIME YOU LEFT YOUR HOUSE?

411
WOULD YOU RATHER BE A GOAT OR NEVER GO ANYWHERE AGAIN WITHOUT BEING CHASED BY A GOAT?

412
WOULD YOU RATHER HAVE THE ABILITY TO PUKE OUT FLOWERS OR HAVE FARTS THAT SMELL LIKE FLOWERS?

413
WOULD YOU RATHER USE HOT SAUCE AS EYE DROPS OR DRINK A BOTTLE OF VINEGAR?

414
WOULD YOU RATHER LIVE IN A REAL LIFE HORROR MOVIE OR LOOK LIKE A CREEPY CLOWN?

415
WOULD YOU RATHER STICK YOUR HAND IN A BUCKET OF WORMS OR A BUCKET OF ANTS?

WOULD YOU RATHER QUESTIONS 4 EVERYONE
GROSS & CRAZY EDITION
NOW AVAILABLE ON AMAZON!

Made in the USA
Monee, IL
31 August 2021